The Next Level You

The Parallel Journey

Tamara D. Brown

THE NEXT LEVEL YOU- The Parallel Journey Copyright © 2021 All rights reserved— Tamara D. Brown

Please direct all copyright inquiries to:
B.O.Y. Enterprises, Inc.
c/o Author Copyrights
P.O. Box 1012
Lowell, NC 28098

Paperback ISBN: 978-1-955605-09-0

Cover and Interior Design: B.O.Y. Enterprises, Inc.

Printed in the United States of America.

Dedication

I dedicate this book, my very first book, to Danielle, my first born affectionately known as Madi. Had it not been for you asking me, when you were in 2nd grade, how much longer it would be before I had a regular job and when you could sleep in your own bed at night, I would have probably drug my feet or would have never quit the Corporate America life-working nights, holidays, and everything in between. Thank you for speaking your mind and always telling me how you feel. I love you.

I also dedicate this book to the TamB. Fitness Community, past present and future members. We're more than a gym, we are family, and I am my sister's keeper. Thank you for trusting & allowing me to do life with you and stretch you in ways you didn't know you could bend.

Of course, this book is dedicated to entrepreneurs and to every person on their journey to their next level in life and business. I know this book will support and add value to your transformation, time and time again.

Acknowledgements

This book would not have been possible without the unwavering support of my husband Reggie Brown. Through my uncertainties, tears, and nonstop work ethic, you never let me quit and reassured me that "we" were ok. Your sacrifices have not gone unnoticed, and I am forever indebted to you. Thank you for your selflessness throughout this journey, I wouldn't want to go to the next level without you.

Thank you to the amazing women who served as role models, trail blazers, & mentors who have encouraged me in invaluable ways. I am grateful for your tenacity, fearlessness, advice, correction, and laughter. I appreciate you sharing your gifts with me.

Table of Contents

INTRODUCTION

How you do one thing is how you do everything. -Origin Unknown

Dear Reader,

You see in the words of the great Langston Hughes, "life for me ain't been no crystal stair." So, if you picked up this book looking for answers or strategies to grow as a person, scale your business, or even if you only picked up this book because you wanted to support or thought it would be a good read, you made a great choice. I know it will support you in more ways than one. Throughout this book, I will share with you the principles that I have applied to my life and business. These principles haven't just worked for me. They've also worked for many of the women that I work with. As a result of applying my techniques, these women have been able to elevate to their next level.

As I am writing this introduction, I asked myself, "What do I want the woman reading this book to know right off the bat?" The answer was simple. Reader, I want you to know, Tamara Brown-the person. My goal is that when you encounter me, you will experience a whole life transformation, meaning EVERYTHING about you will evolve. It has been my experience and the experience of those who work with me, that once a woman begins to evolve and grow as a person, she begins to "level up" in every area of her life. In writing this book, I will share with you pieces of me. It is my hope that as I share me, you will see bits and pieces of you in and through my journey and experiences. Furthermore, I endeavor to provide you with framework that will allow you to embrace where you are and reassure you that your best is waiting on you to show up and live life fully in EVERY area so that you can be complete and whole.

Who is Tamara Brown?

Before there was the Tamara Brown, that you affectionately know, love, and support, there was Tamara Simmons, the youngest of 4 girls, who grew up in a single parent household. She was a young adult who became a single parent her junior year in college-GO COCKS! And oh yeah, she wanted to be an English teacher but somehow never made it to the classroom because she feared failing the Praxis exam and never showed up to take the test. Yep, I saw your eyes grow wide when you read that last sentence. THE Tamara Brown that you know or heard about TODAY was NOT always the confident, successful and loving leader, friend, businesswoman, coach, and trainer that you see and read about today. So, how does one who has had all the odds stacked against them, (being a black single parent from a broken home) with a fear of failure have the audacity to try to educate, lead, and help other women grow from where they are to where they want to be? I'm glad you asked.

This is NOT your average self-help or personal development book. This book is a real-life account of how I broke generational curses, healed from hurt, built a 6-figure business, and helped other women become free and do the same. And here's the best part, I did it all while being happily married with two young kids. Whoever said you can't have your cake and eat it too, didn't tell the whole truth. You can have it ALL if you're willing to pay the price. Not many are willing, but you dear reader, you are! How do I know? Because you wouldn't have picked up the book if you weren't hungry for more.

Many don't think it's possible to have it all, but I beg to differ, because the motto I live by which has yielded exceptional success is:

How you do one thing is how you do everything.

The life you desire to live is dependent upon the short term sacrifices you're willing to endure for long term success. The same perseverance, consistency, tenacity, and grind that you possess in one area needs to show up in every area of your life, no exceptions. You already possess everything that you need to go through your current season and progress to your next level you, it just may take some time before you realize that there's more on the inside of you than you know. And if I can be honest, I was just like you when my journey began. I didn't know that I had a next level until I started investing my time and money into books, podcasts, mentors, sponsors, and coaches who encouraged, pushed, supported, and challenged me in my uncomfortableness. I didn't even know how to build a business, let alone help others. Someone had to bring it to my attention, shout out to my best friend Reba Q, who was real enough with me about what I was creating in my business, Not Your Average Trainer®, LLC. She challenged my mind to accept that TamB Fitness was more than just helping people lose weight.

In the beginning, I did not want to accept that there was more to the fitness journey than numbers on the scale and healthy eating. I didn't want to accept it because I didn't want anyone getting close to me. I didn't want to build new relationships, I just wanted to train people, get the results, and move on to the next client. I wanted an assembly line of before-and-afters. I wanted people to know that I was serious, and that there was nothing fun or amusing or friendly about me. I wanted to be seen as the trainer who did not play when it came to getting results. I showed myself friendly, but I didn't want to make friends, because I wanted to keep my hard exterior. I didn't want people to see that I had flaws. I didn't want these women to get close because what IF these women REALLY got to know me... my story, my pain, my hurt, my inadequacies, or the voids I was trying to fill with this fitness thing. But little did I know, the more women who came to me for help, the more women wanted to KNOW Tamara Brown, the *person* behind TamB, and at some point, I knew I couldn't hide behind the brand all my life.

I had no idea that as I unpacked the layers of hurt and uncertainty for myself through my own transformations, I became more approachable and visible to the community of women who chose me to help them with their weight. With each layer of self that I shed, my mind, life, and business elevated to the next level. It didn't hit me until maybe 2 years after I started Not Your Average Trainer®, LLC, that my next level was waiting on me, and I didn't even know what my next level looked like. All I knew for certain was, **I wanted more**! I was willing to work for it in the gym, in business, and in life, and I remain committed to the work required to see my next level today. It is indeed a lifelong journey.

In the earlier years of business, I thought my next level was mo money... mo money... mo money, but that was not the case. I remember one of the keys to unlock my next level was to see things differently, and it all started with my client Tierony. She was young, shy, and about 130 pounds overweight. Over the course of one year of working with me, she was able to lose 100 pounds. I was excited and shocked when I got the text message with her scale picture with the celebration emojis! I was excited because 100 pounds is a significant amount of weight to lose, and I was shocked because she was thanking me. I wasn't sure why, when she was the one who was doing the work. Throughout her journey she worked hard, and I began to see more of her personality, discovered her talents, and grew to know more about her and her family, like the fact that she's a twin. So, before the text message, celebrating her scale victory, I saw, nurtured, encouraged, and supported who she was becoming and how she was flourishing as a result of her transformation journey with me.

It took for me to see someone else transform and go to the next level to identify that my next level wasn't about money. This momentous victory allowed me to identify or become aware there is more to me, life, and fitness than what meets the eye or what shows up on the scale. I shared all of that to say, it's not by accident that you purchased this book. You picked up this book, because you either had an eye-opening experience like I did with Tierony, and several other women I've worked with, or you feel stagnant in business or life and are REALLY ready to unlock your next level by any means necessary. Or MAYBE, just maybe, you know that there's greater purpose deep on the inside of you and you want to continue growing and learning as you develop into the Next Level YOU, God has called you to be. Either way, the next level you is waiting on Y-O-U and I'm excited to be a part of your journey.

Now, let's get this party started! Be sure to grab a pen or pencil to take notes as you read (in the book in the margins or in between the lines if you have to) because each chapter will help you identify and understand how I saw fitness as the bridge that connects me to my next level mentally, physically, financially, emotionally, and spiritually. I will also breakdown how fitness will help you determine which area in life you've neglected to put in the time and effort to develop, like you may have in other areas, and how it could cost you your next level. Let's Go!

LIFE APPLICATION

The Next Level You is an inside out job!

There's no more fake it to you to make it, and there's no more mask, when you're striving to become the next level you. I remember the day that I was called out by a fitness enthusiast who I became acquainted with on social media. She messaged me one morning after I posted a picture of my breakfast on Facebook and the message said…. "Really quick, can I give you some feedback about your breakfast?" I said yes, PLEASE! And she quickly typed, "No yogurt, no chia, flaxseed oil, 5 oz egg whites and 6 oz of veggies, Facetime me and I can tell you more."

That was the call that changed the game for me. On that call, she got real with me. She told me you're putting in the work in the gym but not in the kitchen. Your body is NOT changing because of your diet. I was shocked, I thought I was doing good. I was eating all the healthy foods that are supposed to promote weight loss: egg whites, yogurt, fruits and veggies. When Kim contacted me, honestly, I was confused and frustrated with the whole weight loss and working out journey. I didn't know enough about nutrition which meant I didn't know how to eat for the body goals and health I desired. All I knew at that time in my journey, was to work out hard in the gym, lifting weights and doing cardio. If I can be honest, I knew what it took to lose weight, but I didn't know or understood what it meant to transform.

That phone call shifted my mindset about fitness, and ultimately started my journey of transformation. On that call, Kim was very informative, but she made me realize that as a leader and gym owner, and for someone who calls themself Not Your Average Trainer, I was being average. I was trying to help others change, but I looked the same. I wanted my clients to get results and post side by sides while I hid behind the camera.

Kim was the one who called me *out* to call me *up* in my fitness journey and challenged my mental fortitude. By the time we ended the call, I was now a nutrition coaching client of Kim's and for the next 3 months which turned into 6 months, I followed her instructions but there were bumps in the road. Those bumps challenged the way I thought, acted, responded, and valued myself. It was in this journey that I developed mental toughness.

CHAPTER 1:
MENTAL TOUGHNESS

"For as he thinketh in his heart so is he…" Proverbs 23:7 (KJV)

Mental Toughness starts in your mind. "Mental toughness, as defined by Mental Toughness Inc., is the ability to resist, manage and overcome doubts, worries, concerns, and circumstances that prevent you from succeeding, or excelling at a task or towards an objective or a performance outcome that you set out to achieve." Whether you are building a business, losing weight, being a wife, motherhood and maneuvering through the cares of life REQUIRES that you build your mental strength. Each level you progress to will require more strength and mental fortitude.

In order to become *the next level you*, you must be mentally sound & tough! When women work with me, the first thing I assess is their current state of mind. I ask questions that give me insight on how they think and perceive themselves. I listen carefully to what words she uses to describe her current health and physique. How does she talk to herself about herself? All of that matters, because in your journey to *the next level you*, you WILL have to FIGHT to keep your negative and self-limiting beliefs and thoughts at bay! And that is NOT an easy feat. I'm not saying this to discourage you, but to prepare you so that you not only win the battle in your mind, but you also win the war on your journey to the next level.

Throughout my journey with Kim, she always demanded more from me, week by week. More consistency with my meal plan, more minutes of cardio, more reps, more sets, more weight, more hustle… every time I weighed in, she wanted more of the current me to die and more of the transformed me to emerge. And just when I thought I had no more to give, and how hard it was to drop that weight and not give into the snacks, I thought about my life and how I'd already overcome.

Graduating from college after becoming a single parent was hard. I thought about how being the only female in my department on my corporate job was hard, but I worked even harder to get promoted. I thought about how I did NOT want to disappoint someone who took the time to call me out because they saw something greater in me and I wanted to see it too.

Mental toughness for me was birthed from the days, and months of telling myself that I was born to defy statistics, that's just what I do, because I didn't want to be a statistic. I didn't want to be another one of the girls from Broad River Road who never went on to become something other than somebody's baby momma. I wanted to prove everyone wrong. I wanted to prove to everybody who ever doubted me that I wouldn't be a statistic. I wanted to show the people who thought I was crazy for leaving my corporate job to start a business and even the people who "slept" on me that I was better than my circumstances. Most of all, I wanted to prove myself wrong. I wanted to get rid of all the doubt running through my mind that I could indeed help these women lose weight, transform their bodies, AND build a 6-figure health and wellness business that catered specifically to women.

I not only wanted to transform my body, but I also wanted to transform my life, because deep down, I knew I was capable of accomplishing much more than what life had already shown me. I wanted to transform my life and the lives of others. I wholeheartedly believe that this journey; the countless hours sweating in the gym and the weekly meal prep days in the kitchen works. Knowing this journey works meant more than the 30lbs I lost or the new look I gained. Deep down I wanted this transformation because I had something to prove. I wanted to prove to my family, the people watching and hating, and to myself that there was NOTHING average about me.

Positive Affirmations

The number one thing I learned during this season of my life (and the thing you need to grasp) is that I needed to establish daily positive affirmations. It can be challenging to be mentally tough when you're constantly beating yourself up through your negative thoughts. If you want to keep your mind strong, if you want to build mental toughness on your path and journey to your next level, you must overcome the self-limiting beliefs that are holding you back. You must realize one major truth; self-limiting beliefs are thoughts not facts.

It's simple to recognize self-limiting thoughts. Self-limiting thoughts are thoughts that come to mind when you are trying to accomplish something great. When you are trying to go to your next level self-limiting thoughts do not line up with what you need to do or how you need to maneuver to your next level. We counteract self-limiting thoughts with positive affirmations. You need to establish three positive affirmations that you repeat loudly to yourself every day. These affirmations should be about you, your business, and your health.

When I work out, the thoughts that go through my mind, come from DJ Khaled.... "All I do is win, win, win no matter what." Some days my thoughts come from ET the hip hop preacher, "When you want to succeed as bad as you want to breathe, then you'll be successful," "You owe you". I took the time during this journey to only listen to or focus on those things that encourage me to reach my goal, so that on the days when "the struggle is real" I can pull some motivation from my mental toolbox and get the job DONE.

In business, when it comes to my ability to train and help women get their desired results, I confess boldly that *I am NOT YOUR AVERAGE TRAINER*®. When I am faced with challenges building the brand or my business, I repeat the following to myself, *I am building a multimillion-dollar company.* When it comes to your health instead of saying, "this is hard" or "I can't do this" say the following sentence out loud and as often as you need to.

"I embrace challenges, because they help me build character and I am taking the necessary steps to improve my health and quality of life."

Write your 3 I am affirmations below, then begin the practice of reciting them aloud daily. The more you say them, the more you'll embrace and execute within them.

1) _____

2) _____

3) _____

Positive affirmations only work when you apply them. You have to be filled with positive affirmations about yourself and about your next level for you to build mental toughness. You must be able to counteract every negative thought with a spoken positive affirmation. Every time you <u>think</u> something negative, <u>speak</u> something positive aloud. Say it to yourself enough times and you will wholeheartedly start to believe it. Then, keep saying it until you see it. Mental toughness is a BIG part of your journey and next level, the level after that, and all of the next levels to come. It is the foundation from which you will build. It empowers you to continue growing, evolving, and transforming.

When it comes to mental toughness and negative thoughts you must get rid of the all-or-nothing attitude. The all or nothing attitude is a concept where you think in extremes. Either you win or you lose; there's no gray area, it's black or white. If you allow the all-or-nothing thinking to rule your mind, you'll be on cloud nine when you succeed, but you'll beat yourself up when you fail. Acknowledging the gray area in between will allow you to see success more often and it will help you celebrate your small wins. In order to build your mental toughness, you need to recognize and celebrate your small wins on the journey to your next level. An important part of mental toughness is finding positivity in every situation. We never lose… either we win, or we learn.

Rest

The second strategy you need to honor to build mental toughness is to recognize when you need to REST, so you don't QUIT. As I was building my mental toughness on the journey with Kim, I was willing to accept any and all challenges she threw at me. I was not going to allow this journey to defeat me. I was goal chasing until Kim said, "building muscle but over doing it on cardio will not give me the body I want!" I was SHOCKED! But it was then that I learned the importance of REST. Kim was real with me. She told me straight out that I needed to slow down because I was going to burn out. She said "Tam, your body isn't trained for this. You must do this gradually, not aggressively."

Think about it, I only turned it up towards the end because I had something coming up (a bodybuilding competition) but I just didn't do this to be doing it. Kim continued, "You can lose weight at the same pace by decreasing your intensity. If your body is not conditioned for intensity it's going to get fatigued and you may open yourself up for injuries, so slow down in order to speed up. If you can't do this day in and day out don't do it. It burns up your muscle and you are trying to build muscle."

WOW, my mind was blown!

Burnout is a REAL thing! I don't care how passionate you are or how much you enjoy doing something. Burnout oftentimes makes us quit or take longer breaks than what we really intend. If you find yourself in a cycle of starting and stopping, or you're the person who has a lot of unfinished tasks, that is a sign that you have not prioritized or included REST as a part of the journey. You may even think that rest will slow you down, but believe it or not, rest will refuel and rejuvenate you to do and be your best.

Oftentimes in the weight loss process, especially when we are new or starting our journey, we tend to go so hard the first few weeks only to find that, after a while we are tired and no longer have the same enthusiasm we had in the beginning. This is true for entrepreneurs as well. Not including rest in our plan and journey is very similar to a child fighting sleep, they become whiny, cranky, and resist sleep until they are forced to take a nap or go to bed. Do you find yourself restless, grumpy, sad, irritated, or frustrated some days after you've repeatedly burned the candle from both ends? Sounds familiar, doesn't it?

But here's the truth: You'll never develop mental toughness if you're always tired. We all need time to refresh and refuel, so that we can serve from our best place and often in the entrepreneurial space, we will want to quit. Sometimes we slow down, but in the worst cases, we throw in the towel and call it quits. But in order for you to get to your next level, in order for you to become *the next level you*, you have to recognize when you need to rest so that you don't quit. What I've learned after 12 years in the fitness industry is that rest days are an important part of the process. Rest allows us to recover. Rest allows us to refuel. Rest allows us to become rejuvenated, and rest restores our creativity.

Here's how essential rest is. When a new client enrolls in my training program, I encourage them to map out their rest days, to give their body a break, because even though we train to build strength and endurance, our bodies are similar to starting and operating a business. We also need to give our muscles, mind, and body a break from the stress of the new program.

I often encourage my friends in the entrepreneurial space to plan their vacations. I know for me personally; I take one vacation every quarter and at least every six weeks I take a mini weekend getaway that helps keep me sane and keeps me from quitting. One of the telltale signs that you are tired and need to rest is that you lose concentration & productivity.

Have you ever had an experience where you're just not getting as much work done or you're not being as productive as you typically would? Have you been working on a project that you know only takes 2 hours, but now all of a sudden it is taking 6 hours? Oftentimes, as an entrepreneur we work so hard to get to our next level, but in actuality, we are really working ourselves into exhaustion.

As a result of exhaustion, you lose productivity. Instances where we could have finished something in an hour is taking us longer because we're not as focused. We have brain fog and we've lost our concentration. This results in frustration and frustration leads to being overwhelmed. Being overwhelmed makes you feel like you're not good enough or that you can't accomplish anything, and it makes you want to quit. So, I encourage rest days. Even in the best fitness training programs, rest is a part of the program and as an entrepreneur you need to schedule your rest days or rest regimen routine.

Have you ever noticed that sometimes at night you can't fall asleep? It's like you're lying in the bed, but your mind keeps going. That's exhausting as well and will not help you at your next level. We need to be able to sleep and get into that deep REM sleep at night. Often, lack of sleep is like a domino effect. If we can't sleep, we can't focus. If we can't focus, we're not getting work done and now we're feeling behind which makes us want to quit.

Quitting is not an option if you desire to grow into *the next level you*. At your next level, you have to dig a little deeper and you need to be your best self. You can only be your best self when you have had rest and you're functioning at optimal levels so that you can serve at your highest level in excellence.

There are several ways I believe you can plan for your rest, here are my top 2:

1. **Set a schedule AND stick to it**

   As an entrepreneur, especially those who may be just starting out and wanting to gain as many customers as possible, setting schedules with your availability is challenging. I remember in the beginning days of starting and growing my business, I would respond to social media messages, text messages, and emails immediately, no matter what time of day or night they came in. After a while of doing that, I noticed that I no longer had control of my time and I was all over the place trying to work my other task around responding to messages. So, to fix that, I streamlined all inquiries to my email. Next, I set up days and times to respond to emails, so that I would be in control of my schedule and not fight with time at the end of the day trying to get things done that should have been done earlier that day. Setting up a schedule and sticking to it, creates boundaries, frees up your time, and allows you to be proactive, not reactive.

2. **Plan your rest/vacations based on your trends, business needs**

   Plan your vacations out ahead of time, at least the dates. You may not have chosen a destination, reached out to a travel agent, submitted a deposit or booked any of the logistics, BUT the time on your calendar is blocked off from appointments, bookings, etc. Unless it's your million-dollar client, you have NO excuse to why you can't take the time away. Trust me, the work will still be there when you get back and there is always something to be done. Take the REST.

Next Level Reflection

How will you plan to rest?

_____

_____

_____

_____

What are your rest or off days?

_____

_____

_____

_____

When are your vacations?

_____

_____

_____

CHAPTER 2:
PHYSICAL FITNESS

In the fitness industry there's a concept called Progressive Overload. Simply put without being too scientific, Progressive Overload is one's ability to increase the weight or the number of reps that you can lift over time. Over time applying the principle of **progressive overload**, allows the body to increase its ability to meet the demands being placed on it. With that being said, you have to be physically fit for the next level because your next level is going to demand more of you. The only way you'll be able to adapt and be successful at your next level is if you learn and embrace the process of building your muscle through resistance training so you get stronger. The stronger you are, the better you're able to carry the load at your next level.

As a Certified Personal Trainer, when I am training my clients, I apply the principle of progressive overload in various ways. Some of the methods I use are gradually increasing the amount of weight over time, increasing the amount of reps completed in each set, or increasing the amount of sets of a particular exercise. My ultimate favorite is decreasing the amount of rest between each set and increasing the training frequency. As you can see, there are several ways to apply the concept of progressive overload, BUT we never improve or get better by doing the same things the same way all the time. We only improve by working through the resistance. We must not shrink back. Instead, we must apply progressive overload concepts to continue to build ourselves up. We don't progressive overload or get stronger, faster, or better unless we keep applying pressure not regressions. Progressive overload allows our bodies to adapt to heavier weight or helps us build endurance and strength. However, while progressing, remember to give yourself adequate amounts of rest and ensure that you are challenging yourself to handle the weight at your next level.

Fit is your ability to endure

Fit is NOT a look or a certain shape or a size, fit is your ability to endure. *The next level you* will require you to be physically fit. Being submerged in the fitness industry has taught me several things about entrepreneurship and life. And here's what I know to be true, and you can probably look back over your journey and say the same. The entrepreneurship journey is not easy, and life will throw you many curveballs, BUT there are five things I had to grow to understand if I wanted to become the best version of myself. I'm sharing these five things with you and as you read and grasp some of the basic fundamental fitness concepts and how they apply to your life in and outside of the gym, feel free to take out your pen, or highlighter and mark up this book with notes on whichever area of the fitness spectrum you need to improve in to become *the next level you.*

Strength Training

The next level is going to require you to be stronger than you've ever been, or it will require you to build strength. The first concept of fitness that you need to grasp is strength training or for the purpose of *the next level you*-resistance training. Out of all the benefits of resistance training my favorite and the most important concept for the next level of you is confidence. Contrary to popular belief, lifting weights and resistance training will not make you look muscular like a man. As women, we do not produce enough testosterone to build or bulk up like a man. So, ladies grab those weights and start lifting so that you can attain the body image you desire.

Confidence in your body image is significant to your next level because you have to show up differently and a lot of times in the entrepreneurial space we shrink back, hide behind the brand, and pass over opportunities because of what we look like. Our physical image at the next level, for your purpose and to gracefully serve those you are called to serve is going to require you to show up! And to show up confident in how you look allows you to show up with confidence and deliver with grace without being distracted about what or how you think the audience perceives you, based on your own weight and body insecurities.

Endurance

The next fitness concept you need to understand is endurance. Most people would consider endurance as cardio or aerobics training. Endurance is the ability to keep an elevated heart rate for an extended amount of time. Now you're probably reading that and wondering why a person, particularly you, would want to do that. Well, the fact is, at your next level and in order to become *the next level you*, you're going to need endurance because the next level doesn't happen overnight. Success doesn't happen overnight and as a fitness professional, who has helped dozens of women transform their bodies, we must understand that with endurance comes patience. Weight loss and transformations do not happen overnight. If they did, everyone would have their ideal body. You have to gain endurance, throughout your journey so that you don't grow impatient or weary in your journey. You have to have endurance so that you don't get tired, you have to have endurance so that you do not give up. Endurance looks different for everyone.

Endurance allows you to go longer with less breaks or breakdowns. Throughout my own personal journey, endurance was the concept that I struggled with the most. I had to learn to endure instead of rushing to the end. I developed endurance by running. I absolutely hate running or any form of cardio except dancing. So, when my coach challenged me to run EVERYDAY, I had to come up with a plan-and that plan was to run 3 miles every other day for about 2 months.

The first time I ran I timed myself to see how long it would take. It took me 53 minutes. I continued running and every time I ran, my time decreased. I was impressed with myself. So much so, that I signed up for a 5K. It was my motivation to do 3 miles in less time. The day of the 5K, I was ready. Mentally, I wanted to challenge myself to complete my 3.2 miles in 30 minutes. I remember that day as a pivotal moment in my fitness journey that taught me a lot about myself.

Throughout the trail, I kept a steady pace. When I would get tired, I wouldn't stop. My mental toughness kicked in, and I talked myself out of stopping by reminding myself about the 30 min goal and how bad I wanted to accomplish it. So, instead of stopping, I would take a deep breath to get my breathing under control and keep pounding the pavement. When the finish line finally came into view, I was relieved!! I increased my pace because I was determined to finish! When I crossed the finish line and saw the clock read 24:53, I could do nothing but jump up and down with excitement! I beat my goal! I never imagined that I would or could run 3.2 miles under 30 mins. It made those days of running worthwhile! Now, I still don't like running, but the benefits are amazing. Because I've taken the time to build my endurance, it doesn't take me as long to do things anymore. I am not as tired; I can go further than before, or I can accomplish more in the same amount of time. How's that for productivity and making the best use of your time?

Building your endurance with aerobic exercise gives you permission to run your race at your pace without comparison or distraction, because everyone is different with differing goals and starting points. What's important is that you strive to get better, to beat the old you every day. If you can continue to endure, you will reach your goals in due time.

Your ability to move and maintain your posture is a part of your next level. When training clients of all shapes and sizes, it's crucial that I assess HOW the client moves or their range of motion when they perform various exercises. It is my goal to have my clients move as far as anatomically possible during any given exercise (full range of motion), because it results in better muscle balance, joint stability, and proper activation of the working muscles, simply put, full range of motion results in overall better movement quality.

Flexibility and Balance

In order to develop your mobility, we must work together to increase your flexibility and stabilize your balance. Flexibility and balance work hand-in-hand because balance requires you to activate your core, the center of your body, for stability. Flexibility requires you to have an increased range of motion. Why are balance and flexibility important for *the next level you*? I'm glad you asked. Balance and flexibility allow you to maneuver through life's curveballs without losing your focus even if you stumble. *The next level you* will move with ease and grace. As you continue to strengthen your balance and increase your flexibility, you'll be able to adapt, pivot, and shift to approach situations, without hesitation, injury, or discomfort. Once you understand how essential mobility is, you'll stop hustling and grinding and execute with ease and grace. Not because you have mastered your craft, but because you now have the skills to maneuver in life and business differently.

For many business owners, balance and flexibility may come in the form of elimination, delegation, or automation. The next level will require you to eliminate distractions and time wasters, delegate tasks that are not directly income producing, and automate tasks that are essential for your business but will allow you to free up your time. Freeing up your time gives you the thing you desire so much, TIME FREEDOM.

Life Application: It amazes me how I am able to relate fitness to entrepreneurship. I have some of my best ahha moments during my workouts. As I'm getting stronger and leaner throughout my transformation journey, I always ask myself how I can become better. How can I increase my performance in the gym and productivity in the office so that I can get more done? The same concepts can be applied to both personal and physical fitness. In order to have balance and flexibility, I had to learn what was preventing me from moving freely and focusing on the things that produce the greatest impact. I took a deep dive and assessed where I was wasting most of my time. And it turns out that I was wasting a lot of time on social media, scrolling down my timeline, with no real purpose, only for entertainment. When I became aware of the amount of time I was wasting, I became intentional about the amount of time I spent on social media by developing a schedule that gave me specific times to engage. That slight adjustment made a significant impact on the amount of time it freed up for me so that I could focus more on income producing tasks.

Another action I took that allowed me to balance my schedule to be more productive in my business and more present in my home was delegating and or outsourcing tasks to my staff. It was definitely tough delegating because it was like allowing someone else to care for your baby, but I knew my staff could accomplish the tasks. Plenty of times I had to tell myself that "it was going to be ok" and that they were going to do an amazing job, in their own way, that aligned with the company values and culture. I had to let go of my desire to do it all. As a business owner who started their business from ground up, I knew that if I didn't get help, I would stunt the growth of my company, and that is not the route I wanted to go. To prevent stunted company growth, I hired 4 women to train and lead a few of the sessions at the gym so that I did not have to be in the studio every time the doors were open. I also hired an assistant to manage the client accounts, emails, and several other administrative tasks so that I can focus on things like marketing, client acquisition, retention, and other streams of income. Although scary at first, it was indeed one of the BEST decisions that I could have made to grow my business.

My most valuable lesson learned through being physically fit, came through the concept of automation. I learned how to efficiently use email marketing to communicate to all of my clients at once and started using automated responses so that I did not have to waste time responding to every email, or inbox message. Automation, delegation, and elimination taught me how to create the balance I wanted in my life.

Flexibility and balance also allow you to improve your posture. I know we're talking about fitness and when posture comes to mind, we think about the way we stand, sit, or the gait of our walk. However, the next level is going to require you to pay more attention to your posture and how your body responds to different circumstances and situations that you're going to encounter. Balance and flexibility allow you to have greater performance. When you can move better and you can control your body better, you will ultimately perform better not just physically but mentally.

Dead Weight

The next concept of being physically fit for the next level is getting rid of the dead weight. When you have unwanted pounds attached to your physical being it makes it harder for you to maneuver. You may feel weighed down or sluggish. Weight loss is a byproduct of a healthier you. When you get rid of unwanted weight you look better, you feel better, and you perform better. These are great benefits. However, the transformation is deeper than that. Being physically fit and getting rid of dead weight will also require you to get rid of the dead weight in your life. That dead weight could be people, places, negative thoughts, self-limiting beliefs, or things that remind you of who you use to be. Remember the old you cannot support you at your next level. Because at your next level everyone can't go with you just like every pound won't stay with you. You've got to be ready, willing, and able to release those unwanted pounds. No matter how comforting or familiar it may feel, you've got to release those unwanted pounds to become *the next level you*.

Training and coaching women to lose weight has given me so much insight on why women recycle those same pounds over and over again. Over the years, I've been able to narrow it down to a few reasons and here are my top two.

1. They are scared of who they will become.
2. They don't believe in themselves.

My training and coaching style is designed to transform not just change. At the very least, transformation will require you to have a growth mindset. Think about it. A caterpillar doesn't become a better caterpillar, it transforms into a new species, a butterfly. The caterpillar must go through metamorphosis, a transformation or change in shape. A caterpillar must go through 4 stages before it develops into a butterfly: the egg, larva, pupa, and adult. Very similar to the process of losing weight.

When I think about this analogy, I think about the work being done behind the scenes when no one is watching. I think about the process at each stage and how it must complete the prior stage to be successful at the next stage. It's all about growth. A caterpillar is limited in its view. Because they can only crawl, they can only see what is happening on their level. Whereas, a butterfly, can get off the ground and fly in the sky. This allows the butterfly to see life from a different perspective.

Let's take this a step further. While the length and weight of a caterpillar can vary greatly depending on its age and type, the average weight of an adult monarch caterpillar is around 1oz. The average weight for an adult monarch butterfly is .50 gram. 1 oz. is equal to 28.3495 grams. An adult butterfly is a fraction of the weight of an adult caterpillar. So, a part of the butterfly's transformation is to shed the "dead weight" it carried as a caterpillar. Undoubtedly, shedding this weight contributes to the butterfly's ability to fly, just as your shedding of your dead weight will assist you as you progress to your next level.

Nutrition

The next concept you need to understand to be physically fit for the next level is your nutrition, what you put in your body. You are what you eat so don't be cheap or processed. Or as I like to say, don't be cheap and watered down. The next level will require you to only operate from a place of quality, value, and support for you to serve. *The next level you* is not only going to require you to evaluate the quality of foods you consume, but also what and who you listen to and see. So, start to think of your nutrition as the foundation of your lifestyle.

Food is the most abused antidepressant. For women, what I know to be true is, we tend to be emotional eaters. We eat when we're happy, we eat when we're sad, we eat when we are out with friends or at social gatherings, we EAT! There is no denying that food brings about fellowship but at the next level, you need to eat to fuel your body, not to feed your comfort. Your nutrition goes hand-in-hand with mental toughness. If you can exercise, if you can build and exercise mental toughness, surely you can control what you put in your mouth.

Your nutrition is an important element of all the components of physical fitness. If you can control what you put in your mouth, employ strength training, add some endurance training, work on improving your balance and flexibility, and get rid of that dead weight, not only will you be physically fit, you'll also be physically sound and on the way to *the next level you*, operating with ease and grace.

Being physically fit is a lifelong journey. All of these things won't come together overnight. It takes time, but that's no different from the path you're on to the next level you. Once you get to your next level there will be another level and a level after that. You never stop learning and growing. When you come to think of fitness as growth and evolution to the next level, you'll think about life and fitness differently, especially if the gym or working out is something you dread.

There are many different ways to incorporate being physically fit into your lifestyle. For most entrepreneurs, we have to commit to an exercise program or routine early in the morning, before we begin our workday. If you're unsure of how to get started or maybe you hit a plateau or simply don't understand how fitness is working for you, I highly recommend that you invest in a certified personal trainer and a nutrition coach. These experts can help you incorporate these areas of fitness into your lifestyle so that you can exercise and apply these concepts to become *the next level you*.

Next Level Reflection

How has your weight/body image prevented you from showing up personally & professionally?

_____

_____

_____

_____

What's one way you can start working to improve your endurance?

_____

_____

_____

_____

What are some tasks that you need to automate? Delegate? And eliminate?

_____

_____

_____

_____

How are you consistently incorporating physical activity into your lifestyle?

_____

_____

_____

_____

CHAPTER 3:
SPIRITUAL FITNESS

The goal is to develop spiritual stamina, so that when challenges arise, you act out of wisdom not your emotions.

Being spiritually fit means that you are connected to something greater than yourself. Spiritual fitness requires you to have and honor a system of faith, ethics, values, principles, morals, and beliefs that provide a sense of purpose and meaning to life. When you use those principles to guide your actions, you are exercising spiritual fitness.

Your spiritual fitness is your internal navigation system. Think of spiritual fitness like your GPS. Every time you travel to an unfamiliar place, or you get lost or have to take a detour/different route, instead of just getting into your car and driving aimlessly, we type our destination address into a GPS to tell us how to get there. In the age of technology, we use google for EVERYTHING, think of your spiritual fitness as your own personal GPS, God's Purpose System.

The next level you will reveal more of your purpose to you.

You may be thinking now how in the world did we go from the gym to the church, lol. Many people think that when they make a decision to lose weight, or get in shape, that only their physical bodies will transform. But that is NOT the case. As you start your transformation journey, you will encounter your inner self, your strengths and your weaknesses. You will become more aware of who you really are, because the journey to *the next level you,* will challenge how you think, feel, and act, your spirit. *The next level you* will require you to embrace who you are becoming and will reveal more of your purpose to you.

Romans 12:1-2 (NIV) states, *Therefore, I urge you, brothers and sisters, in view of God's mercy, to offer your bodies as a living sacrifice, holy and pleasing to God—this is your true and proper worship.*

What does it REALLY mean to offer your body as a living sacrifice? In the aforementioned verse, Paul's words are issuing a call to action. If you're in the entrepreneurial space and you're on any of the social media outlets, any great marketer will tell you that your post needs to have a call to action that drives your market to do something next. For entrepreneurs or business owners, your call to action may be click this link to sign up now. For those who may not be in the entrepreneurial space, when you see your favorite social media friend advertising their product or service and they tell you to share, like, subscribe, or join; that is the call to action. I believe in this particular verse, Paul's call to action is to urge kingdom-preneurs to offer their body as a living sacrifice in the form of a commitment to take action over your health, body, and ultimately your purpose. The goal is to develop spiritual stamina, so that when challenges arise, you act out of wisdom not your emotions.

Let me take you back. Now I'm no Bible scholar, but over the last 10 years or so during my many transformations, I've learned how to use the Bible as a guiding force not only for life but for business. So, check this out… in the beginning or shall I say since the beginning man has always had an unhealthy relationship with food. Follow me now, as I connect the dots for you. Let's go back to Genesis. You know the Adam and Eve story, the fall of man, and the forbidden fruit. To summarize Genesis, chapter 2 verse 17, God specifically told Adam not to eat from the tree of knowledge of good and evil. But then came Eve who was deceived by the serpent. The serpent told her; you won't die if you eat that fruit from the tree. What's going to happen if you eat the fruit is that your eyes will be open to wisdom. The serpent told Eve that she would be like God knowing both good and evil.

Man, so much can be unpacked from the creation and fall of man as it pertains to your spiritual fitness and your next level in life and business. If you look closely at Genesis chapter 2 verse 16, you can see or read that spiritual death occurred. When spiritual death occurs and man seeks self-fulfillment, servanthood is dead.

Often, in this entrepreneurial journey, after we discover our gifts, talents, and skills, we move on to monetize those things thereby forgetting that the core of our business, ministry, and purpose is servanthood. We get into the marketplace and forget just like Eve did. In Genesis 3:6, Eve saw that the fruit was pleasing to the eye and that it was desirable for gaining wisdom. She forgot her call to servanthood and followed the deception of the serpent because of what she saw. We often forfeit the next level because we're deceived by what we see in the marketplace, and we want to monetize more than we want to serve.

When I started Not Your Average Trainer® LLC back in 2014, I knew nothing about business. I knew nothing about client attraction, marketing, or monetizing my gifts and skills. However, what I did know was how to serve. Many times, we think that our next level is going to be about making more money and getting more clients. You may feel volunteers work for free, the game day experience, or even the clout, but I served my way to six figures. I served my way to my next level.

This type of service requires a sacrifice. *The next level you* will require you to go beyond what you see and dig deeper as you rely on your GPS. (God's Purpose System) You don't need another coach. You don't need another outline. You don't need another eBook. What you really need to do is go back to the beginning and recall what God told you to do. Then ask yourself am I really serving? Am I really alive, awake, in tune spiritually, and making sound decisions based on purpose backed by God's word, or am I making decisions to only secure the bag?

Now I'll be honest, TamB. Fitness has had its ups and downs financially. We didn't go straight from 0 to 6 figures overnight, in 2 years, nor 3 years, but we got there and it's only by God's grace and His mercies. We got there through serving! To this day, we've given numerous discounts, free services, and more. Plus, I need to point out that we're in the south which is the home of everything soul food and anti-workout. TamB Fitness grosses six figures through memberships alone. At the time that I'm writing this book, we haven't launched merch, the TamB Fitness collection apparel line. We haven't launched coaching services. The book hasn't even hit publication, neither has our corporate wellness program. The success of TamB Fitness is a direct response to doing what God told me to do and serving! So yes, your spiritual fitness, *the next level you*, will require you to serve.

More recently, entrepreneurs are no longer separating ministry and the marketplace because ultimately the ministry is in the marketplace. I found out in the beginning stages of TamB Fitness that many of my clients did not have a relationship with Jesus. I learned that for some, I was the only Bible that they'll ever read. That's when I knew that TamB Fitness Studio, the actual brick and mortar, was a cover-up to allow women who were seeking God, but unsure of how to seek Him, a place to come with no judgement to be shown the love of God and restore their faith. So, if you think that *the next level you* is only about you, you're sadly mistaken. Your business will more than likely hit a plateau until you learn that lesson, until you restore your heart to the position of servanthood.

What does all of that have to do with my next level? How do I apply it? I'm glad you asked. Let me tell you my personal story about how I discovered fitness as an act of worship. This act of worship would draw me nearer to God, which ultimately drew me nearer to purpose, so that I can operate at my next level and be the best version of myself.

I remember struggling to lose weight. I'd be working out and eating right for about 3 weeks and all of a sudden, I'd lose my mojo. I'd go through this cycle for years, until one day something clicked for me, or maybe I just got tired of fighting myself. Either way, the light bulb came on. I was in a fight between who I am and who I wanted to become. Does this sound familiar? Can you relate to that internal struggle? That's when I made up my mind that who I was had to die in order for me to become all that God called me to be.

You know the saying, starve the flesh, feed the spirit? Now I've searched the Bible for this exact scripture and did not find it, but it made sense to me since Galatians 5:17(NIV) says that the flesh and spirit are in conflict with each other! If I put more energy into the person I needed to become by growing my mindset, improving my self-talk, and honoring my beliefs, I'd get closer to my purpose.

As a trainer, I meet women from all walks of life. One of the major things that these women who want to improve their health have in common is a need to fill a void, to have a greater sense of self, purpose, value and worth. So, they set out on a journey to "focus on me". Have you ever gotten fed up with the chaos of life, felt lost, or wanted a greater sense of purpose and just said, "I'm doing this for me" and really set out to focus on you? That's what I did. That's what I decided. I decided that I'd take the same determination, discipline, consistency, and effort that I put into my workouts and meal prep and apply it to Tamara the woman. I decided to focus less on the results and more on the process, the things I do daily to get the results. I made this shift in hopes that it, the process, would lead me closer to my purpose.

Well, I already said it's easier said than done and I found that out when I got bored with fitness. Well, maybe bored isn't the right word. Let's just say the gym wasn't it for me anymore. I got to a point in my journey where working out no longer took me to a place of worship. It used to give me peace. It used to be my go-to, and then one day it wasn't. I considered this long and hard. I thought, well maybe if I do a different workout, maybe if I change the time that I work out, maybe... just maybe I'd go back to that secret place that gave me peace. That place was a source of creativity. I longed for it but could not find it. The place I was looking for, the place where I find God, was not in the gym. It was not in the sets and reps, in the scale, or new physique.

I remember clearly the day when God spoke to me. "Schedule me like you schedule your workouts. "Schedule prayer and time with me like the time you put in the kitchen when your meal prepping." To me, that was a hard blow. It's almost like He came for me. Even as I am writing, I can honestly say I struggled with this piece, with this spiritual piece of my transformation. Actually, that's not completely accurate. The truth is, I basically just avoided it.

Have you ever felt like you know what to do, you have all the tools and resources to do what you need to do, but deep down inside you're scared of what or who you are going to become? Yeah... that was me. So no, it wasn't a struggle. It was more of an avoidance because I know me. I know, based on my transformations, if I really put in the work, if I put in the time and effort, if I really gave God 120%, I be transformed. What held me back from going all in was fear. This was a type of transformation I knew nothing about. I know how the body works. I know what will happen if I eat certain foods and do certain things. I know what the results of my efforts would be. There's no hidden, or unknown options. 2 + 2 will always equal 4, in that regard. But a spiritual transformation... at that time, I had no idea what that would look or feel like.

A good friend of mine, who also just happens to be a pastor, said to me at the beginning of the year, "Tamara your transformation is going to be a spiritual transformation." I don't even think she remembers telling me that, but I remember because I tensed up when I when she told me. My personal growth and development coach also told me to schedule time in my calendar. She instructed me to block off when I pray, meditate, and when I worship daily. She wasn't telling me anything I didn't know. She was reinforcing, maybe even confirming, what God had already told me to do.

I dare to say that the spiritual transformation is harder than any other transformation I've ever experienced. It's me fighting against me. It's me going into a place that I don't necessarily dominate and I'm not necessarily in control. That's what I'm scared about. It sounds cute to say, "Lord have your way," until you really allow Him to have his way. Letting God have His way means walking into unknown territory trusting that what is unseen will be better what you already know. That is scary, no matter how spiritual you are.

Because I'd never had a transformation like this and I was hungry the change, I started to get really intentional about spending time with God. Here are a couple steps I took. Now is it the end-all-be-all? No. This is what I did, and this is what I'm doing. I bought a new journal. I created a space in my home and made it my no kids, no distractions space. My space is simple, containing only a couch, a blanket, and a bookshelf. I set a daily alarm on my phone and blocked off the corresponding time on my calendars. When the alarm went off, I stopped what I was doing and went to pray. After I prayed, I waited to see if I saw heard from God. That was a new experience for me. In the past, I would walk into a space having my own agenda. I'd know what I was going to do, how I was going to do it, and what the outcome would be. I was accustomed to being in control, but this was one area of my life I had to relinquish my control. I had to give God permission to take control.

Since I had no idea what a spiritual transformation was supposed to look, sound, or taste like, I asked God to introduce me to my fullest potential. I invited Him to remove the blinders from my eyes so that I could fully see my purpose. I asked God to unplug my ears so that I could hear clearly from Him about my next move whether it's personal or professional. Then, I asked God for the biggest thing... I asked Him what He wanted me to do. For the first time, I didn't talk to Him about my agenda. Instead, I asked God to reveal who He wants me to become and who He wants me to serve. Finally, I surrendered to whatever His response was going to be. I submitted fully to God by acknowledging I'm okay with what He wanted for my life.

The greatest initial shift I saw was my mindset and a great group of friends who believe in me and want to see me do well. The mindset was the biggest thing that I had to shift because I really couldn't see how I could obtain a spiritual transformation. I just thought my daily prayers were enough. I was content with the bare minimum, going to church, listening to the word, paying my tithes, and doing the right thing. I thought all of that was enough until I remembered when God told me that I'm Not Your Average Trainer®. For me to live up to what He called me, I needed to know, understand, and grasp everything that God placed in me. I had to fully commit to being Not Your Average Trainer®.

Becoming who God said I was, required a mindset shift. Have you ever had a conversation with someone who just "spoke your language"? It seems like everything they say makes more sense because they "get it". The two of you can vibe because you're speaking the same language and understand where the other person is coming from. That's what happened when God told me to spend more time with Him like I do at the gym. I fully understood what He was calling me to when He said, "Spend time talking to me like you spend time in that kitchen meal prepping so you can get this physical goal for this physical world. Let's talk about changing that time into time with Me." God wasn't asking me to give up what I was already doing or to abandon my other areas of transformation. He was asking me to create time in my day to do it all. His request made perfect sense to me.

I started with baby steps, just 5-10 minutes of time solely dedicated to me being in His presence. That amount of time may not seem like much, but it was vital to my spiritual transformation because it allowed me to download what I needed to live on purpose. Those sacred moments helped me clear my mind and gain creativity concerning my clients, so I'd know who needs what. And that's just the surface... the tip of the transformation.

The next level you is about strengthening your thoughts about your belief in self, increasing your confidence in self, and fulfilling your purpose. Just like lifting weights helps strengthen your muscles, fosters growth, and transforms your exterior, your spiritual fitness works and dwells within you. The next level is about you really operating in and honoring your purpose.

As you operate in your purpose your ideal clients will be easily attracted to you. You will be able to help them solve their problems or heal them from their pain points with ease. If you find yourself stagnant in your transformation journey or in your entrepreneurial journey, ask yourself are you operating in the full potential of your purpose? Are you focused on the things that add value to you and those you are called to serve?

When I started my business, I kinda sorta felt like I was in purpose but honestly, I had no clue what I was doing. I knew that I liked to exercise in an unconventional way; flipping tires, carrying sandbags, pushing past my limits, and really seeing what I could do or how I could push my physical limits and mental strength. I knew it made me feel good and my toned physique was an added bonus. I had NO idea that it would draw women of all ages and sizes to me to help them get fit and transform in a way that they never imagined.

When I quit my job in Corporate America to build my own business, all I had was a vision of what TamB Fitness could be. It was a pretty blurry vision in my head, but nonetheless, a vision of women coming together encouraging, supporting, and motivating each other to push past their mental & physical challenges and go after the transformation that they always wanted. But in order to help them transform, I knew that I'd have to help them break down self-limiting beliefs and mental barriers that had caused them to give up in the past. I also knew my own growth and transformation would be required.

I believed that if I just kept working to grow and improve my mental and physical health, no matter how many times I wanted to give up, the vision of TamB Fitness would become clearer. A clearer vision meant I would be able to train and coach women with confidence. I would no longer second guess myself or my ability to help these women lose weight and have the ultimate transformation experience that would change the way they see themselves, and ultimately their lives. Six years later, not only is the vision clear for me, other women and men see and support the vision as well.

My commitment to my own growth was the most essential element of the growth of TamB Fitness. See, the cycle of weight loss/weight gain will end when you stop fighting yourself and embrace who you are becoming so that you can serve at your next level and look good doing it!

What does spiritual fitness LOOK LIKE??

Spiritual Fitness looks different for everyone because core beliefs vary greatly from person to person. However, for the most part, spiritual fitness looks like being intentional about your thoughts, patterns, and lifestyle. Spiritual fitness doesn't necessarily look like a church. Spiritual fitness can look like anything that ministers to the heart of a person. It also looks like meeting the needs of others.

When I started to build TamB Fitness, I had no idea that what I was building was a ministry for women. I always knew or felt like women needed a place where we didn't have to be anyone but ourselves. I always felt like women needed a place to let their hair down and have conversations that they may not be able to have in the boardroom. I wanted a place where we didn't have to wear masks, a safe place to be true to ourselves. Our journey is what really matters to us the most. With that in mind, I created a space for women who wanted to regain control of their life as well as a sense of identity and purpose. I wanted to build a place, a community, a Sisterhood that would make women do an internal examination of themselves and ask themselves, "Am I living? Am I doing? Am I being everything that God called me to be?"

Since the foundation of TamB Fitness, I've always prayed that the women who come through the thresholds will get what they need to be healed, whole, and fulfilled. I often say don't let this gym fool you, it's just a cover-up. It's just a distraction to get you in the place that will propel, encourage, and inspire you to live full out in your purpose. Don't get distracted by the gym setting because what we're doing at TamB Fitness is ministry! No, it's not a church. No, I'm not ordained as a minister. I just happen to be the chosen vessel that God chose to use to help his women carry-out and birth purpose.

Women give birth. That in itself is powerful. Whether that's physical birth or spiritual birth, women give birth. I've seen it happen over and over again during the last six years I've been in business. Women who come to TamB Fitness who have previously had trouble conceiving begin working out and being consistent in the physical, then they conceived and gave birth in the spiritual. I've seen women who struggled with naturally conceiving conceive after they commit to working on being the best version of themselves. It may start in the gym, but the manifestation is in the womb. For some women, they never physically give birth, but they birth passion. They birth purpose and that propels them to their next level. Spiritual fitness is important to your transformation journey and your next level because it connects you to a greater purpose outside of yourself and gives you a deeper understanding of yourself, if you continue in the process.

Some of the women I've worked with developed a saying, "TamB Fitness more than a gym." It took a while for that saying to grow on me, but as the years passed and I witnessed women transforming their bodies, marriages, and careers, I started to own that what we were doing inside of the four walls of TamB Fitness had much to do with women being exposed to themselves. These were women who knew that there was more in them, women who were ready to see different, not just for their life, but also for their families.

It wasn't a coincidence that the women who came to receive training services saw and felt there was more to this fitness thing than what meets the eye. When starting a fitness journey, most women just think about the weight they want to lose or their desire to be in better health. Most women don't consider what has to be repaired and uprooted before they can get rid of dead weight. Many women come to me with great goals to lose 20, 30, 40, 50, or even 100 pounds, but most of them are not even aware that the weight they want or need to lose has nothing to do with the scale. The scale is often the easy part. These women needed to dig to the root of the issues that caused them to gain the physical weight. The weight was connected to their mindset, self-perception, and the hurt they've picked up on the journey of life.

It has been my experience that before women can start to lose weight with me and my program, I must do damage control. Here's what define as damage control. People think that working with a trainer is going to get the miraculous results instantly. They do not realize that when they present themselves, their current condition, and their goals to their trainer, that trainer has to tear down every fad diet and mental block that they've ever created about losing weight and being healthy. Most people don't know that when they meet a new trainer, that trainer must not only assess them physically, they must also repair and reboot the person's metabolism as well their mindset. This helps to ensure the individual not only loses the weight but gains the necessary tools to keep it off.

What I challenge my clients to do, is to think about all of the deadweight that they've been carrying up until the point that they met me. During our initial consultation, they tell me about all of the things, trainers, and programs that they tried previously and how it worked or didn't work (but clearly it didn't work because they wouldn't be there talking to me). After I gather my notes from their consultation, I'm able to make a clear diagnosis of what's getting in their way. It's very rarely connected to the food they eat or the physical movement they're not doing. Don't get me wrong. Your nutrition, the foods you put in your mouth, and physical movement plays a major role in losing weight but often the first weight that you need to lose is the weight that some of us have been carrying around for years and years… and years.

I have a client that I've been working with for a little over a year and I knew from the moment I met her that she would be an absolute pleasure to work with. She was excited. She had her goals written down. She came to our consultation with a notebook. She was eager and asked great questions. I gave her the plan. She showed up to workout month after month after month. She kept recycling the same 235 pounds. After a while, I started to notice her pattern. She went up, she went down. She went up, she went down. Her weight was in the same yo-yo cycle many people have experienced. I'm willing to bet you've been there before too reader.

After a while, she got frustrated as many of us have. She brought her frustrations to me and said, "I don't know what's going on. I don't know what's wrong. I'm following the plan and I'm coming to the workout. This isn't working." I replied, "I know, but if you are following the plan and you are doing the workouts you should see results unless something else is getting in the way."

Most women don't realize that their weight is emotional and can fluctuate based on their hormones. Many also don't realize the amount of stress they carry from day to day whether that's from being in the corporate space, being a mom, or being an entrepreneur… women carry a lot of weight. We play a lot of roles. We wear a lot of hats. We've learned to operate at a high level of stress. So, in order for me to help this young lady reach her goal, I had to coach

45

her on her mindset. I had to coach her to identify the thing she hadn't dealt with.

You see, the things you need to deal with in your life, the pain, grief, and stressors become added weight that adds to your physical weight. After coaching this young lady through a mindset shift, she quit a job, got some counseling, really started being consistent with following her nutrition plan. And wouldn't you know it, she started to lose weight and her body started to transform. Was it magic? Nope! Did the plan change? Nope! Did we do anything extra? Nope! All we did was deal with the matters of her heart. We dealt with identifying the deadweight and releasing it. Releasing the deadweight that for so many years kept us from living our full potential releases us to shed the excess pounds that are weighing us down physically.

Understanding your why

When I talk to potential clients for the first time, one of the questions that I always ask them is why. Why do you want to lose weight and why now? The same thing applies for you and business. Once you understand your why, you'll understand who you're called to serve because not everyone is your client. When you unpack your why, you unpack your life's experiences. You uncover those experiences that cause you pain and trauma. Once you have been able to triumph and overcome those experiences you will attract clients who have similar experiences so that you can help them overcome. Essentially, your road to triumph becomes a roadmap for your clients to follow. To uncover this roadmap, you must become intentional about uncovering your why.

Get Connected to/Network/WiFi=Holy Spirit

Exercising spiritual fitness so that you can grow your faith muscles in life and business is critical to *the next level you*. One aspect of spiritual fitness that I believe is sometimes taken for granted is your connections your spiritual connections, divine connections, your relationships, and business network. As you are doing the work to become the best version of yourself, *the next level you*, God will connect you to people and resources better connected to your purpose. Think about it, in the great book there are several mentions of connections. Scriptures such as *when two or three are gathered* (Matthew 18:20) or how *man should not be alone* (Genesis 2:18) reveal God's heart on the matter of connections. Even still, He goes on to further demonstrate His thoughts regarding divine connections and covenant relationships by presenting illustrations of those connections through the examples of Ruth and Naomi (Ruth 1:17), David and Jonathan (1 Samuel 18:3), Elijah and Elisha (2 Kings Chapter 2), and Paul and Timothy (Acts 16:1-3). These divine connections brought people into their destiny. Divine connections really are God inspired relationships to remind us that we are not alone on our journey, and that He will provide. They also remind us that we need others because they have something we need so He can give it to us through them to get closer to our purpose.

Two people are better off than one, for they can help each other succeed. If one person falls, the other can reach out and help. But someone who falls alone is in real trouble. -Ecclesiastes 4:9-12

When I think about TamB Fitness, I think about all of the people that I have been connected to over the years to help me build what is now a six-figure business. I can't take all the credit, because when I started, I knew nothing about business. I knew nothing about physical fitness. I just knew that I was fat and fed up. I remember I had a friend from church who introduced me to her trainer. When I started working out with them, she stopped. I continued to work out with him and the relationship she introduced me to ultimately helped me transform because he trained me to become a certified personal trainer. God can and will use relationships to connect you to the next level. Let's not stop there. God used a good friend of mine to introduce me to my first ever business coach who helped me scale my business. I would have never thought about investing in a business coach had it not been for her.

Let's talk about relationship and being connected inside of TamB Fitness. I already believed that with my personality type I'm a connector. I like to connect people to other people and hope that it adds value to their life. So, at TamB

Fitness what I discovered was that my clients and members are connected not only just to me but to each other. I've been able to connect my clients who are looking for houses to realtors, those who are looking for doctors to doctors, and those who are looking for therapists to therapists. I like to say when it comes to TamB Fitness, everything we need is in the house because we're divinely connected.

I also believe that a large part of being connected and staying connected, not just to people, but to God allows you to operate at a different level and do business differently. Remember your GPS? Your God Purpose System, which operates by the Holy Spirit, will tell you when, how, and where to do things. You know what else happens when you have God-ordained connections? You'll have God opportunities. Divine connections and divine opportunities represent new connections, greater connections, new doors, and new seasons. Reader, I want you to pause right here and shout aloud, next level connections!

Spiritual Fitness is the greatest (FLEX) muscle you can develop. The benefits are plentiful. Divine connections are sent to help fulfill what God has ordained, your purpose. There's nothing like exercising your spiritual muscles so that at any given moment you can connect to the Creator just like you would connect to your wireless wi-fi. Your spiritual fitness goes everywhere with you. There is no off/on switch and oftentimes you don't get to pick, choose, or refuse when you get connected. There have been times when I've gone to the grocery store or out just in public and my phone automatically connects to the public Wi-Fi access without me having to do anything. Just having my phone on my person and being in that place connected me. To make divine connections, orchestrated by God, all you have to do is stay purpose and He'll connect you.

Just like any other muscle, spiritual fitness is something you must consistently work on because you want your connection to be strong. These connections to people and resources, or the people that have access to the resources you need, are there to encourage, support, celebrate, empower, and pray for and with you, to help you prepare and excel at *the next level you*. So, all you have to do is remember your why, maintain a servant's heart, and value your relationships, and God will continue to connect you.

Next Level Reflection

What is your why? Keep it simple & straight to the point.

_____

_____

_____

_____

_____

Who are the 5 people you surround yourself with the most? List them.

_____

_____

_____

_____

_____

Think about the 5 people you listed. How does each one of these people connect you to a deeper sense of your why or next level? How is your connection to them beneficial to their next level? If you don't know, ask them.

_____

_____

_____

_____

_____

What are the 3 ways you are using physical fitness to deepen your understanding of your spiritual fitness?

_____

_____

_____

_____

CHAPTER 4:
FINANCIALLY FIT

"Money isn't everything, but it ranks up there with oxygen." - Zig Ziglar.

The next level will require you to know your numbers. How will you know where you're going if you don't know where you are? That's a metrics principle that can be applied in all areas of life and business. *The next level you* will require you to be financially fit, or at least have a plan of action and or strategies for you to be in a better, or the best financial position as possible.

Oftentimes as an entrepreneur or small business owner we are looking to grow, scale, and expand our business which equates to increased revenue, but our financial structure hasn't been successfully established from the beginning. I learned financial fitness the hard way... that's until I learned how to make it make sense for me, which is what I will do in this next chapter. I will help you grasp a deeper understanding of key aspects of the importance of financial fitness.

Growing up in the south there was a couple things you just didn't talk about: sex, religion, and what brings us here to chapter 5, MONEY, MONEY, MONEY, MONEY... MONEY as The O'Jay's so eloquently put it. I got my first job when I was 15 years old working at CiCi's Pizza. No one talked to me about it, no one taught me about it, and I didn't see it advertised to me about how to have a healthy relationship with money. All I can recall is my mom telling me is that you need to either have a lot of money or really good credit because what you can't get with cash, you can get with credit and vice versa. What you can't get on credit you can get with cash.

When I was 15 working at CiCi's, I was just working to pay my cell phone bill, keep gas in my mom's 1993 Ford Escort that she occasionally let me drive because I had my provisional license, and to buy the occasional lunch when I skipped school. Money to me was an act of exchange. If you work, you can get what you want, and if you didn't have enough, save up until you do. My mom also said if a man doesn't work, he doesn't eat. I believe that's in the Bible somewhere too. So, from 15 up until recent years all I knew was work, as a matter of fact when Rihanna came out with that song *"Work, Work, Work, Work, Work"* I knew that she made that song for me, because that's all I knew how to do. I was in my late 20's when I learned that instead of just working for money, I should make my money work for me.

"Profits are better than wages." - Jim Rohn

Now when I heard that quote, I had no intentions, nor had I ever thought about becoming an entrepreneur. As a matter of fact, I only heard that quote because I joined a supplement company called AdvoCare with some very good friends of mine who pretty much talked me into, not just buying the supplements, but being a distributor. I'm grateful that they "bugged" me about joining. See my friends Reba and Calvin had been AdvoCare distributors for about 2 years and for at least one of those years, they kept nagging me about becoming a distributor. At that time, I wasn't interested in becoming a distributor. I wasn't interested in making more money... said no one ever. I just wanted to use the products and get great results. Well, as a result of me using the products and getting great results, I earned additional income, because people always asked about my results and how to lose weight, etc.

Unbeknownst to me, I indirectly started getting mentored, not just by them, but some of the other leaders in the organization. Now most of these people in the leadership team of AdvoCare didn't look like me nor did they sound like me. It was initially intimidating and uncomfortable, but these leaders all had something in common and it was that they wanted to see you excel and live

51

the life that you've always dreamed of. They all knew that type of life required money, lots of it.

It's been said that if you help enough people get what they want, you will get what you want. This saying is why I'm still an AdvoCare distributor. Yes, the products are great, but that's not what caused me to fall in love with the company. I'm still with AdvoCare because of the culture in the leadership. AdvoCare exposed me to people willing to help me understand how to make passive income, the importance of building financial stability, profits, and resale. As I stated, the products are great, but I fell in love with the growth culture, and how freely these leaders would share information and strategies to help you overcome mental, financial, and weight loss barriers.

This unintentional stumbling upon financial mentorship was when the pieces began to click into place for me. All of it started to make sense. Money, weight loss, fitness... it all clicked. Now I'd be lying if I told you I made millions of dollars selling products, I didn't. But it showed me money is a tool that can and should work for you. Exposure to the AdvoCare culture helped shift my mindset which allowed me to establish my finances so that I'd never be broke another day in my life. I learned about investing, profits, and the return on your investment, as well as, how to structure and balance my everyday finances.

They say knowledge is power, but applied knowledge is REALLY the power. The lessons I learned by being connected within this organization allowed me to apply the strategies that were given to my finances, health, spirituality, emotional well-being, and to all other areas of my life. I'll share some of that with you in hopes that as you're reading it, it will click for you as it did for me. As you read, think about your own personal finances and your transformation journey in life and business, so that as it begins to click and make sense for you, you can immediately begin applying what you are learning.

Becoming financially fit will allow you to move from being an entrepreneur to being a business owner. Being financially fit will also allow you to grow from building a brand, to building a company, and will ultimately give you the time and financial freedom that you desire.

Financial Fitness involves the process of learning how to successfully manage, exchange, and responsibly use monetary currency. Money plays a critical role in our lives and not having enough of it impacts health as well as your overall business performance. Financial pressure is repeatedly found to be a common source of stress, anxiety and fear for a lot of people, in businesses and relationships, including entrepreneurs. Remember, how you do 1 thing is how you do everything. So, the same way you achieve your fitness goal or any other life goals, is the same strategies you want to use to accomplish your financial goals.

Just as it is essential to be physically healthy, it is also crucial to ensure that you have sound financial wellness. How can we achieve this? This goal is achieved by doing what we can to ensure that we are not spending more than we make, avoiding debt, and making our money work for us by diversifying our income. Pretty much like being physically fit, achieving financial fitness is a process that requires your attention and complete focus. But what does it mean to be financially fit? It is the ability to cope with all your expenses and live your life the way you want, without any financial worries-the American Dream, right?

Being financially fit will help create goals for each season of your life and business. This helps you in being a more organized person and will also pave the way to success, personal wealth, and generational wealth. The keys to long-term financial fitness are awareness, acknowledgement, and commitment.

Similar to when you start a weight loss or transformation journey, one of the first things you need to do is to establish your financial goals in as much detail as possible. Know how much you make and know how much your recurring monthly expenses are, so you don't have more month at the end of your money. To operate at the next level, you need financial literacy, support, cash flow, and wisdom.

Build a budget

Knowing your numbers includes knowing your profit margins, knowing your business trends, and investing in ways or opportunities to make more money.

Budgeting allows you to create a financial plan by setting goals and working to achieve those goals. A budget will help you in life and in business to determine priorities and as a result, you'll exercise better control in your spending which ultimately yields to more money in your pocket and higher profits for your business. Also, a budget will allow you to be better prepared for large purchases and investments and to help you identify and explore new opportunities.

Financial fitness is VERY similar to nutrition, or at least the way I teach my clients when they are striving to reach their body goals. When I talk to my clients about nutrition, most of them are really shocked that there's a difference between eating healthy and eating for your goals just like there's a difference between making money and investing money. Money is a universal language and for the most part, it's understood at the very basic level. So, when I talk to my clients about their nutrition, specifically a caloric deficit and macronutrient splits- protein, carbs and fat, I relate it to their bank account. To set up a budget, you must simply identify expected revenue (cash coming in) and expenses (cash going out). At the very minimum, most of us know how to either balance a checkbook or prevent our accounts from going into the negative, i.e., overdraft. We understand that language, so I apply it to nutrition. I tell my clients every day, you're going to get a deposit of x amount of calories and each day you have to spend those calories in different denominations. This analogy has helped my clients understand, here's an example for you.

Each day Tamara receives 2000 calories in her nutrition bank account. Out of those 2,000 calories, 300 has to be spent in fat, 1200 has to be spent in carbs, and 300 has to be spent in protein. That's how you have to spend your nutrition account every day. If you go over, you gain weight. If you don't spend it all, you lose it. You don't get to make it up another day. When I explain this concept to my clients and help them understand that their nutrition is just like their bank account, we often discover there's room for improvement not just with our nutrition, but with our finances.

When you can break a concept down to its simplest form to help someone understand on their level and their paradigm, they begin to connect the dots.

It's going to take a lot of trial and error, a lot of planning, and maybe even some variety for many people to balance their nutrition in a way that produces long-term sustainable results. I wasn't really good with money, to be honest, there's more room for improvement. In my early twenties when I was just barely making it trying to make ends meet, I knew what needed to be paid and I knew what I could make arrangements on. Some things have a higher priority than others, like your mortgage, light bill, water bill, and other essentials. It's like protein, carbs, and fat- the essentials macronutrients.

One of the reasons why I struggled as an entrepreneur early in my business is because I really didn't understand my numbers. I wanted to treat my business like I treated my personal life. I tried to pick and choose which bills I'd pay, and which ones would allow me to make payment arrangements, but that got old really quick. I didn't have my priorities in line, and my bank statements showed it. Most times when people start businesses, they offer their products or services at a deeply discounted rate. They try to get as many clients as they can because in their mind, if I can get x amount of clients at this amount, I can afford this rent, cover this bill, etc. They start the business doing whatever it takes to cover the basics but forget they also have living expenses. At least that's what I did in the beginning.

In my mind, I did the math like this: I need x amount of clients so that I can afford my studio rent. Then after rent, I need X amount of clients for utilities. As long as that made sense and as long as I hit those numbers, I was good. At least that's what I thought until I kept going home broke. I had a studio filled with women, but I was broke. It couldn't wrap my mind around where the rest of the money was. I did that for several years and got fed up, burned out, and tired of chasing people for pennies on the dollar to pay bills. That's when I really started to look at budgeting differently.

Instead of looking at budgeting like many of us look at diets, like what we can't do, what we can't eat, or what we can't have, I started to look at budgeting as a plan of telling my money where to go and what it would do. It all made sense when I could look at it in a nutrition perspective. When you learn about staying within your calorie boundaries and how to creatively use those calories to make up your protein, carbs, and fat, you start wondering how you can make your nutrition work with foods you actually like. You become creative as you find ways to add in foods without causing a caloric overdraft.

So that's how I started looking at my personal and business finances. I put things in place so that I wasn't spending more money than necessary. I was also able to plan ahead for emergencies, big purchases, and future investments without breaking the bank or going without things I wanted or needed. I got rid of the rob Peter to pay Paul mentality and started structuring my personal and business finances the same way I structure my day-to-day nutrition plan. How I got results in the gym and results in my body, was also the way I'd get results in my finances, and you can too. With a plan, you understand and can execute consistently.

Credit

It is important for you to have good credit NOW and at your next level- your credit, personal and business credit history and scores are a reflection of how well you honor your commitments. Credit tells everyone whether or not you did you did what you said you were going to do. Credit also allows you to leverage and expand your reach in places where cash cannot take or sustain you. Credit will allow you the opportunity to receive something that you may not have the cash for right now, with good faith that you would be able to repay the debt when the time comes. Credit buys you time.

Credit gives you a track record, and a paper trail to lenders. It puts your character on display. When you get to your next level, the last thing you want people to do is question or attack your character. Clean up your credit so when you need it you have it, and no one can challenge it. If you need help improving or building your credit, seek a reputable company or someone you trust to assist you in the process. There are many online sources that can guide you with different ways to help you build and or repair your credit, but just like anything it will require work. It will require your attention to even the smallest of details. I prefer to do it myself so that I can learn in the process versus hiring someone to do it for me and then not knowing how I really got into the predicament.

Throughout my young adult years, I was mindful about my credit and my credit score, but I also knew how to leverage my credit. If I didn't have the cash today, I'd charge it but by the time the bill came, I made sure I'd have the cash to pay the bill. For some people that works well, and for some people it doesn't. You just have to be aware of the amount you're charging, so you don't get out of control and bite off more than you can chew.

Credit often has or gets a bad rep. People would like to tell you that credit is bad, but what I know to be true is, if you don't know how to use a thing, you will abuse a thing. Most people abuse credit because they're not taught how to build, manage, and leverage it. Below I'll give you a couple credit basics that worked and are working for me, that you can go and check out and apply them to your finances. Keep in mind that I am a FITNESS & NUTRITION expert, so seek professional financial advice if you're in way over your head.

There are many types of credit, but the most common two types are installment loans and revolving credit. Installment loans are like your student loans, your car payment, and your mortgage. Whereas revolving credit is a line of credit that you can keep using after you've paid it off, so that's like your Victoria Secret card, your Nordstrom Rack card, or your Belk card. Both types of credit have their pros and cons. Most people focus on the cons, so do your research.

All Americans get a free credit report every year, yet some people don't even know what their credit looks like because they're scared. They know they didn't pay XYZ but it's important for you to be aware of what your character looks like on paper to the banks. You need to know your credit score. Your score is like an indicator of what your trustworthiness is on a scale of 300 to 850. There are at least three reporting agencies: Experian, TransUnion, and Equifax. The higher your score, the more likely you'll be approved for new credit or offered a lower interest rate. Many factors are used to determine your credit score which you'll probably see referred to as your FICO score.

Credit Agencies take our payment history into consideration. They are looking to see if you kept your previous commitments by paying on time. Your credit score also takes into consideration the amount you owe on your accounts Many people refer to this as your utilization ratio when it comes to your revolving credit. Your utilization ratio compares the amount you owe on your credit card to the credit limit on the account. You want to aim to use 30% or less of your available credit on each account.

Your credit history also plays a factor in determining your credit score. Creditors want to look at your history. Typically, they want to see how well you kept your word over a length of time. Anyone can pay on time for a month or two, but creditors want to see if you've kept your financial commitment for the last few years. It's important for you and your business to have good credit. Having good credit means that you are making regular payments on time, on each of your accounts, until your balance is paid in full. Bad credit means you're having a hard time holding up your end of the bargain. Maybe you were late on a payment. Maybe you didn't pay the full minimum balance due. Bad credit is like bad news or gossip, it will travel far, and it will have detrimental effects. Negative information such as late payments or collections generally stay on your credit report for at least 7 years. So, the next time you go apply for a credit card or get a loan, make sure you can keep and honor your word or it may have a negative impact on your financial future.

How to Save

I never really understood the point of saving until I became an adult and had to pay my own bills. I'm a part of that millennial generation, you know... YOLO. You only live once. So, if I only live once, why am I saving? Carpe diem, seize the day! C'est la vie, this is the life! All of that sounds great until you get a flat tire, or your hot water heater goes out in your house, or you get an unexpected emergency bill. Then the savings gets real. I was never really big on saving money. I mean when I was working, I think I'd save like $20 a month, basically $10 out of every paycheck. Then I met my husband, who had some very old school ways with money. I'm talking money in the mattress under the bed type of ways. Now my husband, he's a saver. It's a high priority for him. He has a savings account, and his savings account has a savings account. The only thing that I was really taught about saving was to save up for a rainy day.

I've read books on how to budget and how to save. All of that seemed like music to my ears until I realized that in order for me to save, I'd need to stop spending so much or make more money. There was a time when both my husband and I decided to become entrepreneurs at the same time. Oh, I don't know whose idea that was, but we got the message real quick! Somebody has to have some stable income. Both of us being entrepreneurs and neither one of us really knowing how to be an entrepreneur that makes money was a bad idea. Whatever savings I had; I ran through. Whatever savings he had; we ran through. We both were looking at each other wondering what happened and what would be next.

I'm very fortunate that he went back to work, and I pursued Not Your Average Trainer® in the months to come. After that experience, I was able to really see the benefits of having money in emergency savings. Some people say they can't afford to save. I say you can't afford not to. When you have a savings account or an emergency savings fund, things like a flat tire or a new hot water heater are no longer emergencies and aren't stressful situations. Here are a couple of strategies I did to start and build my savings accounts. Yes, that's savings with an s, because I'm saving for all sorts of things, emergencies, trips, Christmas gifts, etc. You can save for whatever you want, just don't spend everything.

The first thing that I did to create savings was actually have a savings account, preferably one that's not readily accessible, like Ally Bank. It's a bonus if it has a high interest rate so that it can make you more money. I had to have a savings account that I did not have access to see every day because in my mind if it is there it must be for me to spend. LOL

The second thing I did was, I automated my savings. Every Friday like clockwork, money will be transferred from my checking account to my savings account. I chose Fridays cause that's payday. You choose any day you want. If it's automatic, it's out of sight out of mind. Also in my subconscious, it reminds me that the money has to be there in order to be transferred. This kind of puts the reins on my spending during the week. Start with any amount. It doesn't have to be hundreds or thousands. Any amount is better than no amount. Start with $5 a month if you have to. That's a little over a dollar a week.

You may be thinking, that sounds great Tamara, but where is this "savings money" going to come from? Start going through your bank statements to find your discretionary spending. This is money you spend that you or your household can live without. Is it Starbucks? Are you paying for subscriptions you no longer need? Is there anything you can possibly spend a little less on? Remember, we're only looking to start with a little more than $1 a week. Search your bank statements to locate that money. When I thought I didn't have money to save, I got rid of my cable, and home phone, and started saving it. Listen to me, the money is somewhere, you just have to find it. If you are making money, then you can save money, no excuses!

Do your investments and goals align?

Being financially fit will help you make better decisions and choices about what you need to invest in. Your number one investment should be yourself. Investing in yourself at a high-level yields exceptional growth and exposes you to people and places that your previous level could not. I remember my first time investing into a business coach. I really wasn't sure what to expect or how much it would cost. All I knew was that what I'd previously done didn't work then and it wasn't working now. I hit a brick wall. I was out of creative solutions, and I needed help.

A good friend of mine suggested a business coach to me. I checked her out and she had great results testimonials. It really seemed like she had the answers and could help me take my business to another level. I attended her free event and of course was pitched an offer I really couldn't refuse. I mean I could, but I didn't want to. I invested $15,000 in a business coach. At that time, I didn't have $15,000, but I was determined to find it because I really believed that her systems and strategies would work for me and my business. But I got so much more than business support and strategies. Investing at this level taught me so much more about myself, how I value myself, and my core beliefs. Not only that, investing in myself at such a high-level gave me the opportunity to be around other women in business who worked at levels that I admired to be. It gave me the opportunity to meet other highly ambitious women, that have elevated conversations around life and business. As a result, my confidence increased not only in myself, but in the service and transformation that I provide to my clients. Having a business coach at a high level also taught me how to package and leverage what I know at premium prices to honor myself and my craft as I reach and work with my ideal client who understood value, not just investment.

For most entrepreneurs, our investments look like a business coach, hiring a team, and serving in a capacity that brings us joy that may or may not be directly related to our business. Your investments should align with your goals. If at any time they don't, it won't produce its greatest return and will not give you fulfillment. The worst thing that could happen on your journey to the next level, is for you to have done the work only to find out that you're on the wrong path. Many entrepreneurs hit a stumbling block in their journey, just like I did when they get caught up in chasing money, and not serving the client. Don't let this be you, become financially fit so that you can serve at your highest level, focusing on delivering value and not collecting a check.

Now I know this is the financial fitness portion of the book and I stated before I am not a financial expert. What I've done is taken my experiences in life and in business from a fitness perspective an illustrated to you how principles and strategies correlate to other areas. Sure, I could have used this opportunity to tell you about stock investments or real estate investments, but that's not my thing. The greatest investment you can make while you're pursuing *the next level you* is an investment IN you. Invest your time, money, and energy where you want to go. But not only that, make sure that you understand the return on your investment. Here are three ways that I invest in myself and have over the years in my pursuit to my next level.

The first way to invest in yourself, is through reading. I have a degree in English. I was so intrigued with reading, but I got a degree in English to help me better understand language in subject-verb agreement, storytelling, and the different parts of a story. Now I read for advancement. It's still an enjoyable way to release stress, but I choose books that give me insight into things that I'm interested in that can propel me forward. I read books about sales, mindset, and business. I encourage you to choose books not just for enjoyment. Instead, choose books that have text you can apply. I know you're thinking, I don't have time to read books. But there are options for busy people like you. There are audiobooks and podcasts. Whichever format you decide, just read, and read daily. Five or ten minutes here and there will make a world of difference.

The second way that I invest in myself is that I take time for me. I'm a wife mom-of-two, and a business owner with multiple service lines. All of those roles require 100% of me. Maybe not all at the same time, but they require a lot. So, in order to continue to perform at my best each week, I take time for myself whether big or small. Sometimes I just watch my favorite TV show, go get a manicure/pedicure, a massage, take myself out to lunch, or sometimes I just close my laptop and play with my kids. Other times I do absolutely nothing. You cannot leave you out of the equation. I put me on my calendar which can even mean therapy sessions with my therapist. The activity I choose is not important. What matters is that I'm intentionally carving 30, 60, or 90 minutes of uninterrupted time for me into my day. You can't pour from an empty cup, and no one who's of importance to you wants your leftovers. Refresh yourself and your body, mind, and loved ones will definitely thank you.

The third way, and this is in no particular order of importance, that I invest in myself is by seeking out opportunities each quarter to invest in something that I believe will help me grow. In the past, I've invested in 12-week financial courses, certification programs, or sometimes I just take the opportunity and hire a fitness coach or trainer to help me see fitness differently. These types of investments allow me to continue growing, build my knowledge, gain a different perspective while I explore me and do the things that I enjoy doing.

There are so many aspects in financial fitness. I challenge you to review your financial health report using the information provided in this chapter. Building a strong financial foundation, allows you to build up your financial portfolio. Everyone thinks that money will solve a lot of their problems, but Puff said, "Mo Money Mo Problems." I've even heard that money will change you, but money is only a magnifier. The more money you make, the more your character will be revealed. If you're stingy while you're broke, you'll be stingy while you're wealthy. If you can't manage the little, surely you won't be able to manage the overflow. It's important that you get it right. There's always room for improvement no doubt about that, but you cannot improve what you ignore or are not willing to work on. So, just like all of your other goals, your financial goals will require you to work, so that when you arrive at your next level, you don't fumble in your finances. Instead, you will be equipped to handle them well, so that you can reap the benefits of being a good steward over your money.

Next Level Reflection

When's the last time you looked at your credit report? Do you know your credit score?

_____

Do you know how much cash is coming in and how much is going out? When was the last time you reviewed your budget?

_____

_____

What is your savings strategy?

_____

_____

_____

What are you saving for? Why is it important to you?

_____

_____

_____

If I looked at your bank statement and saw your last 5-8 transactions, what would your money habits say about you?

_____

_____

_____

Are there any transactions on your most recent bank statement, that you can eliminate and delegate to your savings plan? If so, list them here.

_____

_____

_____

In what ways do you invest in yourself?

_____

_____

_____

Have you dedicated time each week just for you? If not, what day of the week will you dedicate to yourself? What time will you put you on your calendar?

_____

_____

_____

CHAPTER 5:
EMOTIONAL WELLNESS

Emotional wellness inspires you to own your truth, your past and present experiences as you grow and become *the next level you*. It is important to be attentive to both positive and negative feelings and be able to understand how to handle these emotions, so that you can rid yourself of emotional weights. As we discussed in Chapter 3, dead weight weighs you down. When you deal with your "stuff", it transitions from dead weight that holds you back to steppingstones for your next level. That transition will allow you to share your story, your experiences, without shame. Emotional wellness includes self-care, relaxation, stress reduction and the development of inner strength. It also includes the ability to learn and grow from experiences. Emotional well-being encourages autonomy and proper decision-making skills. It is an important part of overall wellness.

"Emotions make you cry sometimes, emotions make you sad sometimes, emotions make you glad sometimes." - H-Town

I guess it all started around when I was 18. This was the age where I could go to doctor's appointments without my parents' permission or them having to escort me or be in the room with me with the doctor. I can't recall what happened, or maybe I can and just don't want to admit it, but I ended up seeing a doctor and later being diagnosed with manic depression, or what we know today as bipolar disorder. I was shocked. I was scared. I was embarrassed, and I didn't have anyone to talk to. This was before therapy was really a thing. I mean it's always been a thing, but in today's society, everyone is actually talking about counseling and therapy. When I went through this experience, these conversations were not being had.

Maybe it was the stress of my parents' divorce, my mom's stroke, me trying to work in between school and ultimately just trying to figure life. Better yet, maybe I was just trying to figure out who Tamara was as she stepped into the world of unknowns which is better known as college. If I can be completely honest, it was like I was any other little black girl from Broad River who was lost, but I was determined not to let that beat me.

I never took the medicine that the doctor prescribed me. As a matter of fact, I didn't even take the prescription to get filled. How could they tell me something was wrong with me? I didn't want to accept it; therefore, I did not accept it, and I'm sure I paid the consequences of it as I continued my journey of self-discovery. Like many of you reading this book getting to know me, Tamara Brown, I've had some traumatic experiences that have left me bruised and scarred, bent but not broken. In the previous chapter we talked about spiritual fitness, but while enduring this eventful season of my adolescent life the only way I knew to escape the pain was to pray, dance, and have sex.

I didn't know anything about therapy or living a Christian lifestyle. I didn't see that lifestyle being lived in front of me. I heard people talk about it, but I didn't see that being lived. I saw sisters dropping it like it's hot and getting paid, both in real life and on BET. So, my view of life and how to manage emotions was different. I grew up in an era, where my parents always said, kids are to be seen not heard and whatever happens in this house stays in this house. Now I'm sure my parents did the very best they could with their resources and knowledge about parenthood. I'm sure they didn't know the damage that was being caused because their intention was to love, not harm.

So why am I telling you this? I'm telling you this because before you can grow, evolve, and even step into *the next level you*, you must confront and deal with all the things that you've tucked away, buried away, or even swept under the rug of your heart. Your purpose... your why... this journey... your next level is about impact. While healing from your emotional experiences will always cause you to see or experience reality through a filter, that filter is different for everyone. You can't possibly make a significant difference in someone's life, make an impact, or leave a legacy worth leaving if you don't deal with the matters of your heart, the messages in your mind, and the voice in your ear. Now we're not going to spend this whole chapter talking about negative emotions and healing, but you will have your good days and you will have your character building or reflection days. The journey to *the next level you* will require you to take your mask off. Everyone wants to be successful or at least everyone *should* want to be successful in life and in business but there is definitely a price to pay.

Emotional wellness is the ability to successfully handle life stresses and adapt to change in difficult times. It may look like a lot of different things to a lot of different people but only you know when you are well. How you feel can affect your ability to perform everyday activities and how you interact with those you are in relationships with. Working with women over the last several years, not only have I examined my personal life, but I have the inside scoop. This position has made me privy to various portrayals of women who are emotionally well and women who aren't. The TamB Fitness community whether I knew it or not then, is a place where women have an opportunity to improve their emotional wellness. In this community, I am able to utilize five "unwritten" strategies to help improve emotional wellness. Here are the five strategies. Grab your pencil to circle or underline where you may need to work on your emotional wellness.

1. Brighten your outlook

You better not be the brightest crayon in the box. In order to brighten your outlook, you must surround yourself with a diverse group of people who may or may not have had similar experiences to the ones you've experienced.

2. Reduce stress

You don't have to tell me it's easier said than done. Stress is the silent killer. Stress can give you the burst of energy you need, but stress can also overstay its welcome which will be harmful. Persistent stress will put you in a constant state of flight or flight. Learning how to cope with and manage your stress will boost your resilience so when tough times come, and they will come, you'll be tougher.

3. **Get some quality sleep**
You must get rid of that hustle and grind mentality, that late night/early morning mentality because *the next level you* will be efficient. In order to be efficient, you have to be well rested. I get everything done every day because I am efficient. You know that long to-do list you have? We often sacrifice sleep to accomplish those tasks. Sleep affects both our mental and physical health. It's arguably the most vital ingredient to your well-being. Sleep helps you think more clearly, have quicker reflexes, and better focus. Go to sleep!

4. **Be mindful**
Being mindful or mindfulness is the trending or hot word today. Mindful meditation, mindful eating, mindfully mind yo business. I'm just playing about that last one, but you do need to mind your business. In the words of the legend Lauryn Hill, *"it could all be so simple, but you'd rather make it hard."* The actual concept of mindfulness is a simple ancient Greek practice that's about being completely aware of what's happening in the present. That means everything that's going on around you and inside of you. Being more mindful requires you to be intentional. It requires you to make a commitment and practice it faithfully. Being mindful means coming out of autopilot mode which is where some of us seem to get stuck.

5. **Strengthen social connections**
Now this is the second time connections has appeared in this book, so it must be some type of important, right? As much as you may want to stay to yourself and despite you feeling as though you are "too grown" to make new friends and build relationships, *the next level you* will require you to strengthen your social connections. Please note that's not only on a professional level. Strengthening social connections means you're developing a healthy and strong support system. You can do things like

get active and share good habits with family and friends, girls' trips, or have meaningful conversations with the people close to you. You can take a class to learn something new and to meet new people, or one of my favorites, volunteer in an area you care about. Social connections are important because if you're doing anything great and you want to make any type of massive impact, you can't do it alone. You need people, a variety or diverse range of people.

Next Level Reflection

Where can you do or what books are you reading to help brighten your outlook?

_____

_____

_____

Identify your top stressor.

_____

What triggers that stress?

_____

_____

What preventive measures can you take to reduce your response to those stressors?

_____

_____

Rate your quality of sleep on a scale from 1-10 with 1 being extremely low quality and 10 being extremely high quality.

_____

What's getting in your way of quality sleep?

_____

_____

How can you improve your quality of sleep?

_____

_____

When will you start implementing your plan to improve your quality of sleep?

_____

What distractions do you need to get rid of to be more mindful, i.e. be in the moment?

_____

_____

_____

_____

How can you strengthen your social connections, your real-life interactions, not social media? Be specific.

_____

_____

_____

_____

CHAPTER 6:
HOW I GOT ALL OF THIS FROM FITNESS

itness is a pursuit of growth and balance. I fell in love with fitness because I fell in love with who I was becoming. This love affair began before I knew who I was becoming, what my purpose was, and what I was called to do. I loved being challenged. I love what it means to transform.

I recently got a tattoo on my left shoulder. It says, *trust the process* and includes a caterpillar, cocoon, and a butterfly. It became clear to me early on in my journey, before there was a TamB Fitness, that fitness took me to a place where I had to internalize and deal with who I truly was at my core. I had to deal with ME, and all of my challenging thoughts, experiences, hopes and dreams… everything!

I often tell my clients, if you can lose weight and keep it off, if you can transform your body, you can do anything because it doesn't start in the gym it, starts in the mind. I knew that if I improved my physical, the quality of my life would improve, and spread like a wildfire. I honestly learned how to navigate life through the lens of a gym, through the lens of fitness like the saving grace. With fitness, the possibilities are endless! You can lift heavier. You can lift lighter. Making one change in how you execute or perform a movement can change the whole dynamic of the exercise. You can go fast. You can go slow. You're in control, and I like control. The whole transformation journey is based on the concept of cause and effect. If I do this, then this will happen. If I do this long enough, this other thing will happen.

Thinking of personal and professional growth made sense to me when I juxtaposed it with fitness. It's a way to let off steam while challenging your physical and mental strength. It's a way to would prove your endurance and increase your mobility and flexibility. It's a way to build your confidence and self-efficacy. There's so much to fitness and being physically fit than what initially meets the eye.

Most people are enamored or in awe when they see women and men with nice physiques, chiseled arms, chest, ABS, nice legs, but what I see when I look at me or someone else who's working on their fitness, is someone who did NOT wake up like this. No shade to Beyonce, but what I see is someone who change their lifestyle for this, got up early or worked out late for this, changed what they ate for this, cried for this, poured down sweat for this, lifted heavy, ran far, and worked on themselves every day for this! I see someone who told themselves, "I was worth this."

This isn't an "I woke up like this" or "what you see is what you get" type of situation. When the women walked through the doors of my gym, I saw so much more than someone who wanted to lose weight. I heard the depth of what the women were really saying when they said, "I want to lose my stomach." I saw women who were really scared but ready to own their truth so they could continue to write their stories. I saw women who were ready to be made whole no matter what size they wore or the numbers they saw when they stepped on the scale. I saw women who recognized everything that has happened to and for them were chapters in their books, but not the end. I saw women who wanted more for themselves and their careers, and they were unwilling to forfeit until they got what they wanted regardless of how physically tired they felt.

The women who walked through my doors were women who were ready to be introduced to their full potential. They were tired of being mediocre or average. Those women were ready to get rid of their self-limiting beliefs and I was the one on assignment to help them connect their dots and make sense of their world through fitness.

You see, their story may not be like mine, but I knew I could help them see things in life differently. So, when I'm asked, "Tamara Brown, what makes you Not Your Average Trainer®?" I don't get stumped. I no longer have to think twice, and I don't second guess who I am, whose I am, and what I'm called to do. I've done the work over, and over, and over again in every area. It may be challenging work, but I did it, I am doing it, and will continue to do the work because I believe in myself. I believe in you, and you have what it takes. You're more than enough and you have everything you need within you.

Thank you for taking the time to read this book to the end. I hope that you saw pieces of you in me. I trust you found value in what I've shared and that this book supports you where you are right now and while you're on your way your next level. It's my truth. It's my story told through my lens and from my experiences that allow me to live out loud and be unapologetically me. My truth empowers me to be free from people and things, and most importantly free to help you become whole and free, or shall I say… have your cake and eat it too.

CPSIA information can be obtained
at www.ICGtesting.com
Printed in the USA
BVHW090426161221
624023BV00015B/1679